The Two Margarets

A Struggle for Christian Freedom

Carine Mackenzie

Published by
CHRISTIAN FOCUS PUBLICATIONS LTD
Geanies House, Fearn, Tain, Ross-shire IV20 1TW,
Scotland

© 1985 Christian Focus Publications Ltd
ISBN 0 906731 437

*To Margaret
in memory of
her mother and my sister
Margaret*

Contents

Foreword			5
Chapter	1	On the Solway	7
Chapter	2	Trouble at the Farm	11
Chapter	3	Unwanted Visitors	15
Chapter	4	Betrayed	19
Chapter	5	The Trial	25
Chapter	6	Reprieved?	30
Chapter	7	No Turning Back	35
Chapter	8	More than Conquerors	38
Chapter	9	'Take another drink'	44
Chapter	10	The Great Reward	46

Foreword

What does the word 'Covenanter' mean to you? Do you think of narrow minded religious fanatics?

The Two Margarets tells a very different story. Here were young Margaret Wilson and old Margaret MacLachlan standing up for civil and religious freedom in the face of real persecution. They valued the simple direct teaching of Scripture and their total loyalty to their Saviour led them to martyrdom. This story is one which appeals to all and touches the emotions in a very telling way.

These two Margarets made the supreme sacrifice for the sake and cause of Jesus Christ, their Lord and Master.

A. Sinclair Horne
Scottish Reformation Society
Edinburgh

(Rev. A. Sinclair Horne is the author of *Torchbearers of the Truth* and *In the Steps of the Covenanters.*)

The Martyr of the Solway — Sir John E. Millais, 1829-96 — Photo courtesy of Scottish Reformation Society

CHAPTER 1

On the Solway

A gasp of horror swept through the crowd of country folk as they watched the fearful sight before them. The rushing tidal waters of the Solway Firth rose relentlessly and covered the head of the young girl, well-known and respected in the district. It was in fact the second such death that they had witnessed that morning.

'What a disgrace. That Major Winram and his men will have to answer for this,' muttered one onlooker.

'Why did the lassie not just say the words they were wanting to hear? I can't understand her — or the old wife either,' added another under her breath.

What was the explanation for this horrific scene on the morning of the 11th May 1685?

The years 1680 to 1685 were very difficult times for the Scottish God-fearing people called Covenanters. The king, Charles II, decreed 'I am the head of the church. All my subjects must worship in the way I order.' The Covenanters believed that the Lord Jesus alone was the head of the church. They wanted freedom to worship God as the Bible taught them and were prepared to fight to win this freedom. The king's soldiers and followers were very cruel to them.

An old man would be reading his Bible in a quiet secluded spot on the hillside. Suddenly a troop of soldiers would swoop down on him, pistols at the ready. If they felt like it, they would not hestitate to kill the old man on the spot.

A young man might be walking along a

quiet country road.

'Where are you going to?' would be the rough question.

'I have some business to attend to a few miles away,' he would reply.

'What kind of business? Perhaps you are going to one of those religious meetings. Give him a beating that he will not forget!'

They seemed to delight in cruelty.

The women, young or old, were treated just as harshly. Many frightened old women who ran away in panic from a troop of soldiers were instantly shot down in cold blood.

The persecution was so ferocious in the years 1684 and 1685 that they were known as the 'Killing Years'.

The old woman and the young girl drowned in the Solway on that May morning were two of those who loved the Lord Jesus above all and wished to worship him as their Master and King.

CHAPTER 2

Trouble at the Farm

Margaret Wilson was eighteen years old. Her father Gilbert was a farmer at Glenvernock, in the parish of Penninghame, Wigtown-shire. He was quite a wealthy man. He grew crops on the good soil and reared sheep and cattle. Margaret, her sister Agnes and brother Thomas grew up in a comfortable home with loving parents.

Both Gilbert and his wife went along with the wishes of the king in matters of religion, but their three children did not attend the ministry of the local curate at Penninghame.

Margaret, Agnes and Thomas would have met together with other Covenanters to worship God and to hear the Gospel preached regularly, but not in a church building. They would worship in the open air at what was called a 'conventicle'.

Word would be passed from one to another as to the safest place to meet on the Lord's Day. Sometimes it would be on a hillside, sometimes in a field or beside the river. Always one or two sharp-eyed members of the company would stand guard at a strategic position to give early warning of any approaching soldiers. At the pre-arranged signal of danger, the congregation would scatter in all directions, praying to the Lord who is a 'refuge and strength and a very present help in trouble.'

Often Psalm 46 would have been sung out in the open air and given comfort to God's people in their trial.

Preachers who had been put out of their pulpits ministered to these people — preaching the gospel and encouraging the

Christians to trust in the Lord for all their needs.

The authorities of course soon found out the people who did not put King Charles first. Much harassment and persecution followed those who put Jesus first.

For Margaret, Thomas and even thirteen year old Agnes home at Glenvernock was not safe.

One day Mrs Wilson was busy in the kitchen preparing food for the family.

The clatter of horses' hooves broke the peace of the country morning.

A proud captain swung down from his horse and strutted up to the farmhouse door. He banged two or three times with his boot.

'Open up!' he shouted. 'The King's troops are here!' Fearfully Mrs Wilson opened the door.

'We want to question Margaret Wilson. She lives here, doesn't she? We have reason to believe that she is not loyal to his majesty the King,' announced the captain.

'No sir, I am afraid you cannot speak to her at this moment. She is not in,' replied Mrs Wilson, trembling.

She was nearly sick with fear. What would the soldiers do to her?

Several soldiers barged past her and noisily searched the house, thrusting their swords behind curtains and under the beds. Disgusted with their fruitless search they stomped out of the house.

'We will be back again soon to deal with young Margaret and your other children,' threatened the captain. 'I order you to inform us when they come home.'

The troop of soldiers clattered out of the farmyard as noisily as they had come in. Mrs Wilson breathed a sigh of relief but the worry was with her day and night.

CHAPTER 3

Unwanted Visitors

Margaret, Thomas and Agnes were forced to escape quietly from their own home and find a safe secret place to hide in the deserted parts of Upper Galloway.

Still the soldiers turned up at the farmhouse of Glenvernock.

'Where is Margaret Wilson? Are you hiding her in here? Search the house!' The house would be searched high and low. Still no sign of Margaret, nor Agnes nor their brother. The soldiers were really angry.

'We cannot punish these young rascals. We will have to punish their father instead.'

Gilbert Wilson was taken to court many

times in both Wigtown and Edinburgh. He was fined large sums of money. The travelling would have been expensive too. Edinburgh was more than one hundred miles away — a difficult and dangerous journey with little prospect of mercy at the court.

One day Gilbert looked up from his work in the farm steading to see a large party of soldiers — some on horseback — some on foot — approaching his farm.

'More trouble,' he thought. 'What can they want now? They must know that the children have not been here for weeks. I had better run inside and warn my wife.' The captain of the soldiers marched to the door.

'These men of mine are needing food and a place to sleep. Get your wife to make enough food for us all — there are about a hundred. The officers will use your beds. The men will just lie on the floor. Find as many blankets as you can.' Gilbert and his wife were staggered at his impertinence, but were powerless to argue.

Mrs Wilson was run off her feet cooking food and serving one hundred rough soldiers who did nothing to help. Far from it — they deliberately broke furniture and damaged the property.

And the expense! But if Gilbert complained the captain only laughed and even more damage resulted.

Gilbert lost a lot of his money at this time. When he died years later, his widow was destitute and had to end her days living on the charity of her friends.

While the parents were suffering at home, Margaret, Agnes and Thomas were suffering out on the hillside amongst the rocks and caves. They had to look after themselves. Food, clothing, shelter — the basic necessities of survival in a Scottish winter had to be begged for. The threat of discovery and possible death always haunted them. Happy memories of home and of father and mother added to their suffering.

But they believed that this suffering was a small price to pay for the freedom they had to worship God.

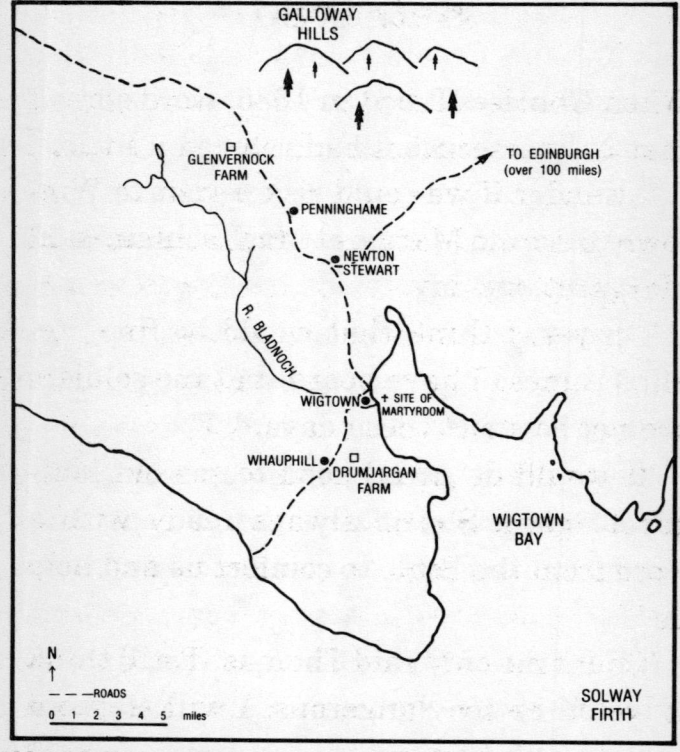

Map of Wigtown area

CHAPTER 4

Betrayed

When Charles II died in 1685, word spread that the persecution had relaxed a little.

'I wonder if we could risk a visit to Wigtown to see old Margaret MacLachlan,' said Margaret one day.

'Oh yes, I think that would be fine,' replied Agnes. 'I have heard that the soldiers are not so strict these days.'

'It would do us all good to see old Margaret again. She is always ready with a word from the Bible to comfort us and help us.'

'Count me out,' said Thomas. 'I still think it would be too dangerous. I will stay out here for a bit longer.'

By now the authorities were offering a reward to anyone who gave information that led to the arrest of the three young people. So Thomas was right in thinking that the visit was dangerous.

But leaving Thomas to fend for himself on the moors, Margaret and Agnes carefully made their way down to the little market town of Wigtown where their dear old friend Margaret MacLachlan lived. Old Margaret was nearly seventy years old, and was a widow. Her husband had been a carpenter living on the farm of Drumjargan. She was a good, plain, honest country woman, full of good sense and faith in the Lord Jesus. She lived a godly life and was a great help to young people like Margaret and Agnes Wilson.

Anyone who was on the run from the authorities because of their religious beliefs would be sure of shelter and food at Margaret MacLachlan's home.

Margaret and Agnes reached Wigtown without mishap. In the town they met a man called Patrick Stuart whom they knew quite well.

'Come to my house for a bite to eat, girls. You must be hungry,' invited Patrick.

'Thank you. You are very kind,' the girls replied.

Patrick put food and drink before them. How good it looked. Before they could take a sip from the glass, Patrick raised his glass high.

'The King!' he toasted.

The girls were quite taken aback. They said and did nothing.

'The King!' repeated Patrick loudly. 'Won't you drink the health of our sovereign the King?'

'No, we will not,' said Margaret modestly, and Agnes nodded vigorously in agreement.

Patrick Stuart immediately left them

and proceeded as fast as he could to the authorities in Wigtown. There he reported on the girls and collected his reward as an informer.

Before long a party of soldiers arrested Margaret and Agnes and threw them in prison — a horrible place called 'The Thieves' Hole'. A few days later they were moved to another prison.

Who should be in that prison too, but their dear friend Margaret MacLachlan. She had been arrested one Lord's Day while she was having family worship in her married daughter Elizabeth's home at Drumjargan.

The soldiers forced their way in and dragged her off to prison where she was very badly treated — she had no fire to keep her warm, no bed to lie on and very little food.

The two Margarets and young Agnes were having a very difficult time. But they were Christians and would be able to take

Ruined building at Drumjargan once used for religious meetings

comfort from the words of the Bible.

They probably remembered Joseph in prison and how life was made bearable because 'the Lord was with him'. (Gen. 39.23.)

Perhaps they were like Paul and Silas singing psalms in prison.

The Scottish Metrical psalms that had given them so much comfort at the conventicles on the hillside would also give them strength in prison.

'This word of thine my comfort is in mine affliction: For in my straits (difficulties) I am revived by this thy word alone.' (Psalm 119.50.)

CHAPTER 5

The Trial

In prison both Margaret and Agnes were asked to sign what was called an 'Abjuration Oath.'

On the 8th November 1684, the Covenanters had written down what they believed. In this document they said that as the Lord Jesus was head of the Church, King Charles did not have the power to make them worship in the way he wanted. They also believed it was wrong that people were killed because they had different religious views to those of the king.

This made the government very angry and on the 22nd November 1684 an Act was passed that required everyone to say pub-

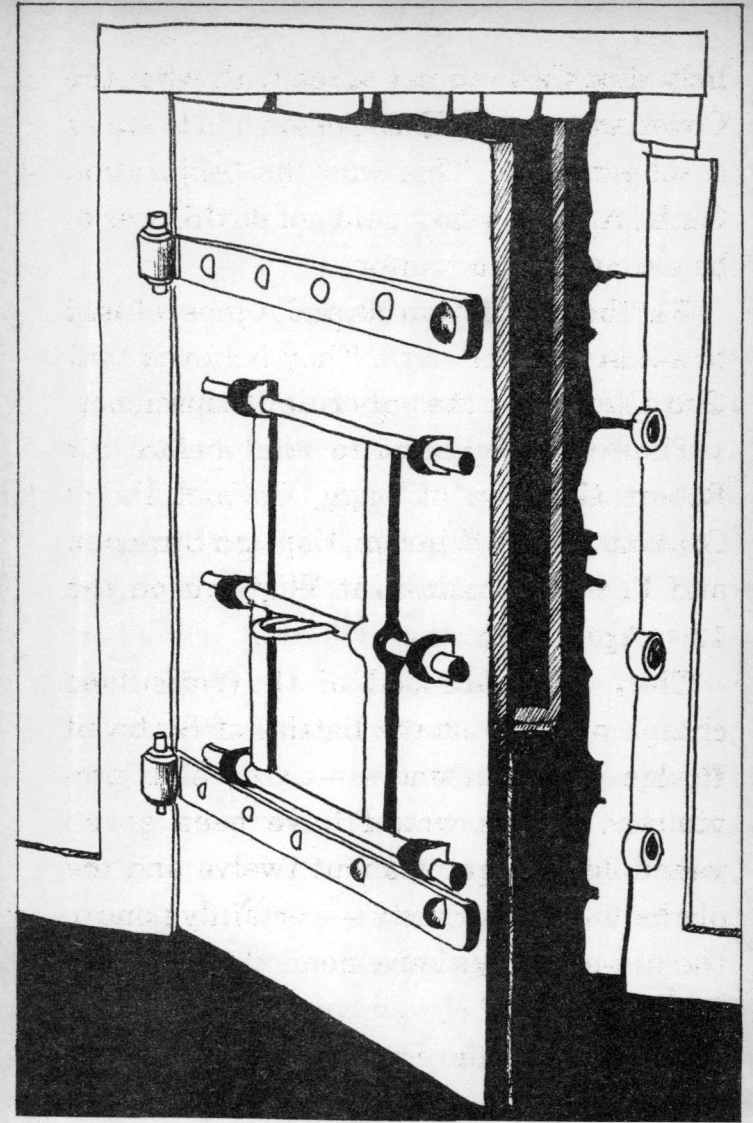

The prison cell in Wigtown Town House

licly that they did not agree with what the Covenanters said. Each person had to swear a solemn oath. This was the 'Abjuration Oath'. Anyone who would not do this was to be executed as a traitor.

But the two Margarets and Agnes refused to swear such an oath. They believed that God's Word was the only rule of conscience.

They were brought to trial before Sir Robert Grierson of Lagg, Colonel David Graham, Major Winram, Captain Strachan and Provost Cultrain at Wigtown on the 13th April 1685.

They were accused of the ridiculous charge of being at the battles of Bothwell Bridge and Airdsmoss — six years previously. Agnes would have been seven years old, Margaret about twelve and the old lady well over sixty — certainly none of them were anywhere near these battlefields.

They were also charged with being at

twenty field conventicles and several home conventicles in private houses. These charges may well have been true but no actual proof was given.

How awful to think that worshipping the Lord was counted a crime.

The women could take comfort in the words of Jesus, 'Blessed are they which are persecuted for righteousness sake, for theirs is the kingdom of heaven.' (Matt 5.10.)

Again the authorities tried to force them to swear the Abjuration Oath but to no avail. Neither arguments nor threats would change their minds.

The women would rather suffer than say anything that would deny their Lord and Master, the Lord Jesus Christ.

At this mockery of a trial the old lady and the two girls were without adequate defence. Even the jury who would decide whether they were guilty or not had been specially selected. A verdict of guilty was passed on all three.

They refused to kneel to receive the sentence but were forced down on their knees.

The sentence was passed.

'On 11 May 1685 they should be tied to the stake fixed within the flood marks in the waters of Bladnoch near Wigtown on the Solway Firth — there to be drowned.'

They listened to the sentence, cheerful and composed throughout. The Lord gave them grace to help in time of need. His promise to them was true as it always is — 'I will never leave thee nor forsake thee.' (Heb. 13.5.) They counted it an honour to suffer for the sake of Jesus.

CHAPTER 6

Reprieved?

The news soon spread round Wigtown and the country districts beyond.

'The two Wilson girls and old Margaret MacLachlan have been sentenced to death.'

'Oh surely not! That's just criminal. They have not harmed anyone.'

'Shush, woman, don't let the soldiers hear you say that. They will be after you next.'

'Poor Gilbert and his wife. How will they stand up to this blow?'

And so the conversations went, among friends and neighbours.

As soon as the sentence was passed, Gilbert Wilson set off to travel the hundred miles to Edinburgh to plead for the lives of his two daughters. As Agnes was only thirteen years old, he was allowed to purchase her release for £100 sterling — a very large sum in those days.

His pleas on behalf of Margaret seemed to touch the hearts of some of the members of the privy council.

'My daughter Margaret is only eighteen years old. She is a good kind girl and would do no harm to anyone. It would break my heart if she were killed. Will you not show mercy? Perhaps some of you are fathers. How would you feel in my place? Let me take her home. Her mother longs to see her. I will pay all I have.'

He left Edinburgh hopeful that perhaps she too would be saved from the terrible fate the authorities had planned for her.

Young Margaret was bearing up very well in prison. She wrote a long and loving letter to her family and friends, assuring them that she was very conscious of God's love for her soul and that she was completely reconciled to whatever God had in store for her.

Nothing would persuade her to swear the abjuration oath just to save her life. The Crown rights of her King Jesus were being challenged. She loved Jesus more than anything and could not deny him.

Some people said the older Margaret was not so brave. A letter was sent to the privy council in Edinburgh pleading with them to change the sentence and saying that she was willing to take the Abjuration Oath, and to conform to the King's wishes.

Margaret MacLachlan was not an educated woman. It is most unlikely that she would have written such a document herself. Probably friends, feeling anxious about Margaret, would have got together to try to save her from the death sentence.

A reprieve was granted by the privy

council on 30th April 1685 to both Margarets as a result of the letter and the appeal from Gilbert Wilson. What a relief to them both and to their families. Surely they would be free now — free from persecution.

Road leading from the cell to the stake

CHAPTER 7

No Turning Back

In spite of this official reprieve, on the 11th May 1685 the two women were taken from the tolbooth of Wigtown to the shores of the Solway Firth, guarded by Major Winram and a company of soldiers. They wanted the Margarets to suffer. They led the women to the spot one hundred yards from the town.

A large excited crowd of spectators followed the execution party.

In between the low and high water marks two wooden stakes were fastened firmly into the sand, sticking up about six feet above the level of the sand.

The two Margarets stood dignified, watching what was going on. We can be sure that their trust was in Jesus who for the sins of his people, like Margaret Wilson and Margaret MacLachlan, was nailed to a piece of wood sixteen centuries before at Calvary. He was their master and example. 'He was led as a sheep to the slaughter.'

'Tie the old woman to the stake nearer the water,' came the order. 'Tie her tightly.'

'We want the young lassie to see her drown. That might frighten her into changing her mind. We'll soon see how brave she is,' taunted the soldiers.

A chill of horror swept through the crowd.

'Yes, the soldiers are going to see it through.'

They helplessly watched the rushing tide advancing on old Margaret. Each wave brought the water up higher — to her feet, then her knees — her waist. Would she change her mind?

Those in the crowd who had no sympathy with the Covenanters' cause could not understand how she could let things go this far.

'What difference would a few words make?'

They shook their heads in bewilderment.

Others in the crowd sympathised with old Margaret and were praying that she would be given the needed strength.

The next wave lapped up to her chest. Would she shout out the words that would free her from the ropes?

No! Margaret was steadfast and courageous throughout. Her Lord and Saviour was with her at her time of need.

The waves were at her neck — then her mouth.

Then it was all over for Margaret MacLachlan as far as this world was concerned, but what a welcome there would be for her in the heavenly kingdom. 'Come ye blessed of my father, inherit the kingdom prepared for you from the foundation of the world.' (Matt. 25.34.)

CHAPTER 8

More than Conquerors

Young Margaret had to watch as at last the waves closed over her old friend. What a sight for the onlookers but how much more awful for Margaret knowing that she was next.

'What do you think of that?' a heartless soldier demanded of Margaret.

'What do I see,' she answered calmly, 'But Christ in one of his members wrestling there. Do you think that *we* are sufferers? No, it is Christ in us: for he sends none into battle on their own.'

As the water came nearer to young Margaret she started to sing some verses of Psalm 25.

Site of martyrdom (at high tide)

'My sins and faults of youth do thou O Lord forget.

After thy mercy think on me and for thy goodness great.

God good and upright is the way he'll sinners show.

The meek in judgment he will guide and make his path to know.'

Then with a calm cheerful voice she repeated these triumphant verses of Romans chapter 8.

> 35 Who shall separate us from the love of Christ? shall tribulation, or distress, or persecution, or famine, or nakedness, or peril, or sword?
> 36 As it is written, For thy sake we are killed all the day long; we are accounted as sheep for the slaughter.
> 37 Nay, in all these things we are more than conquerors through him that loved us.
> 38 For I am persuaded, that neither death, nor life, nor angels, nor principalities, nor powers, nor things present, nor things to come,
> 39 Nor height, nor depth, nor any other creature, shall be able to separate us from the love of God, which is in Christ Jesus our Lord.

She gained strength from fixing her mind on these great truths of the gospel, looking forward to being in heaven with the Lord Jesus Christ. 'Consider him who endured such contradiction of sinners against himself, lest ye be weary and faint in your minds.' (Heb. 12.3.)

She then started to pray. The waters reached up to her lips. Just then the soldiers cut her free. A sigh of relief escaped from the crowd.

Margaret gasped and struggled for breath for a minute or two.

'Will you pray for the King?' she was asked. 'I wish the salvation of all men and the damnation of none,' she meekly replied.

'Dear Margaret,' begged one of her friends, 'say "God save the King", please say "God save the King".'

Margaret responded with great composure, 'God save him, if he will; for it is his salvation I desire.'

Immediately her friend swung round to Major Winram. 'She has said it, she has said it. Let her go now.'

But Major Winram and the others were not satisfied with that statement.

Grierson of Lagg cursed her. He had a cruel temper, and had already killed five Covenanters without allowing them time to pray.

'We don't want such prayers,' he said. 'Make her swear the oath.'

Winram came over to force her. 'Swear the abjuration oath,' he demanded, 'or else you will immediately be tied up again in the sea.'

Without hesitation Margaret replied, 'I will not; I am one of Christ's children; let me go.'

Margaret and her family and friends had their hopes of a reprieve cruelly dashed once more. The women on the shore wept bitterly. Their friend was not to be freed after all.

The town officer of Wigtown took his halbert (a spear with an axe head) and gleefully shoved Margaret into the water again. 'Take another drink, then,' he exclaimed.

Very soon the powerful waters of the Solway closed over the head of the second Wigtown martyr.

The crowd was stunned. What a tragedy they had witnessed that day. But the tragic deaths meant eternal glory for the two Margarets. They were now eternally free.

CHAPTER 9

'Take Another Drink'

What an effect this martyrdom would have had on the onlookers.

Those who loved the Lord Jesus although saddened had seen that his grace is sufficient and that his strength is made perfect in weakness. They knew that their friends had gone to be with Jesus.

Would any of the men in authority be at all stricken in their conscience? We have all one day to give an account of the deeds done in the body whether they be good or bad. These men were no exception.

One, the town officer, who had said 'Take another drink then' had a constant reminder of his cruel remark to the dying girl. He was a broken old man, roaming round the streets of Wigtown suffering from an unquenchable thirst. He could not go out of the house without taking a large jar of water with him. The merciful Lord does not punish us as we deserve, but the locals of Wigtown were of the opinion that this disease was linked to the town officer's part in the drowning of the two Margarets.

The graves of the two Margarets

CHAPTER 10

The Great Reward

When the tide ebbed again, the two bodies were recovered from the sands and buried in Wigtown church yard. Later stones were erected in their memory.

One said,

> Here lies Margaret MacLachlan who was by unjust law sentenced to die by Lagg, Strachan, Winram and Graham and tied to a stake within the flood for her adherence to Scotland's Reformation Covenants, National and Solemn League. 1685.

Margaret Wilson's epitaph was more poetic —

> Here lies Margaret Wilson, Daughter to Gilbert Wilson in Glenvernoch. Who was drowned Year 1685 — Age 18.

MARGARET WILSON, aged 18 daughter of a farmer in Glenvernock,
AND
MARGARET MACLACHLAN, aged 63 tenant in the farm of Drumjargan, both in this County were drowned by sentence of the Public Authorities in the waters of the Bladnoch near this place on the 11th of May 1685, because they refused to forsake the principles of the Scottish Reformation and to take the government oath, abjuring the right of the people to resist the tyranny of their Rulers.
Also
WILLIAM JOHNSTONE gardener and JOHN MILROY chapman in Fintilloch, and GILBERT WALKER, servant in Kirkala, all in this County were summarily executed in the town of Wigtown in the same year and for the same cause.

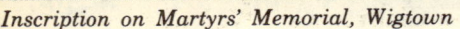

Inscription on Martyrs' Memorial, Wigtown

> Let Earth and stone still witness bear
> There lies a virgin martyr here
> Murdered for owning Christ supreme
> Head of His Church and no more crime
> But not abjuring presbytery
> And her not owning prelacy.
> They her condemned, by unjust law
> of Heaven nor Hell they stood no awe
> Within the sea, tied to a stake
> She suffered for Christ Jesus sake.
> The actors of this cruel crime were,
> Lagg, Strachan, Winram and Graham.
> Neither young years, nor yet old age
> Could stop the fury of their rage.

These two women are fondly remembered long afterwards for the love they showed to their Saviour the Lord Jesus Christ and his cause in Scotland. Jesus said: 'Blessed are you when men shall revile you and persecute you and shall say all manner of evil against you falsely for my sake. Rejoice and be exceeding glad for great is your reward in Heaven: for so persecuted they the prophets which were before you.' (Matt 5.11-12.) The two Margarets received their reward.